Mapping the World

First Guide to Maps

**Marta Segal Block and
Daniel R. Block**

Heinemann Library
Chicago, IL

445654

©2008 **Heinemann Library**
a division of Reed Elsevier Inc.
Chicago, Illinois

Customer Service 888-454-2279
Visit our website at **www.heinemannlibrary.com**

Designed by Jennifer Lacki, Kimberly R. Miracle, and Betsy Wernert

Originated by Modern Age

Printed and bound in China by South China Printing Co. Ltd.

12 11 10 09 08
10 9 8 7 6 5 4 3 2 1

10-digit ISBNs: 1-4329-0795-6 (hc); 1-4329-0801-4 (pb)

Library of Congress Cataloging-in-Publication Data

Block, Marta Segal.
Mapping the world / Marta Segal Block and Daniel R. Block.
    p. cm. -- (First guide to maps)
Includes bibliographical references and index.
ISBN-13: 978-1-4329-0795-2 (hc)
ISBN-13: 978-1-4329-0801-0 (pb)
1. Cartography--Juvenile literature. 2. World maps--Juvenile literature. I. Block, Daniel, 1967- II.
    Title.
GA105.6.B558 2008
526--dc22

                        2007048627

Acknowledgments
The author and publishers are grateful to the following for permission to reproduce copyright The
author and publishers are grateful to the following for permission to reproduce copyright material:
©Corbis pp. **20c** (Arctic, Royalty Free), **27** (zefa/ Jason Horowitz); ©Getty Images pp. **20a b**
(rainforest, Royalty Free; desert, Royalty Free); ©Map Resources p. **4**; ©Superstock p. **6** (Royalty
Free); ©The Bridgeman Art Library p. **26** (John Carter Brown Library, Brown University, RI, USA).

Cover image reproduced with permission of ©NASA.

Every effort has been made to contact copyright holders of any material reproduced
in this book. Any omissions will be rectified in subsequent printings if notice is given
to the publisher.

Disclaimer
All the Internet addresses (URLs) given in this book were valid at the time of going to press.
However, due to the dynamic nature of the Internet, some addresses may have changed, or sites
may have changed or ceased to exist since publication. While the author and publisher regret any
inconvenience this may cause readers, no responsibility for any such changes can be accepted by
either the author or the publisher.

Contents

Any words appearing in the text in bold, **like this**, are explained in the glossary.

What Are Maps?

A map is a flat drawing of a part of the world. People who make maps are called **cartographers**.

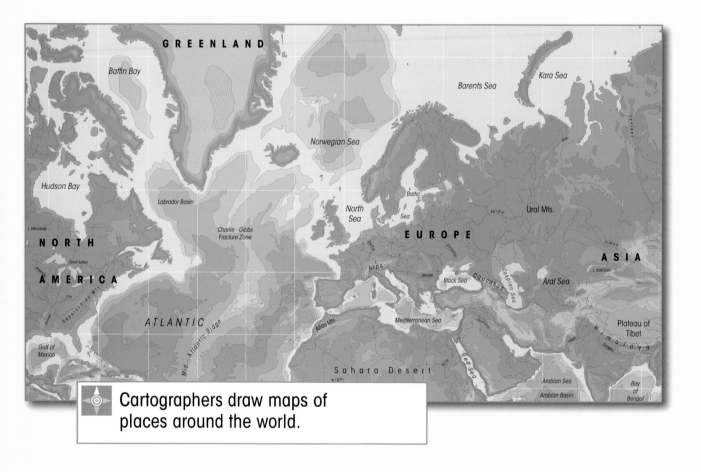

Cartographers draw maps of places around the world.

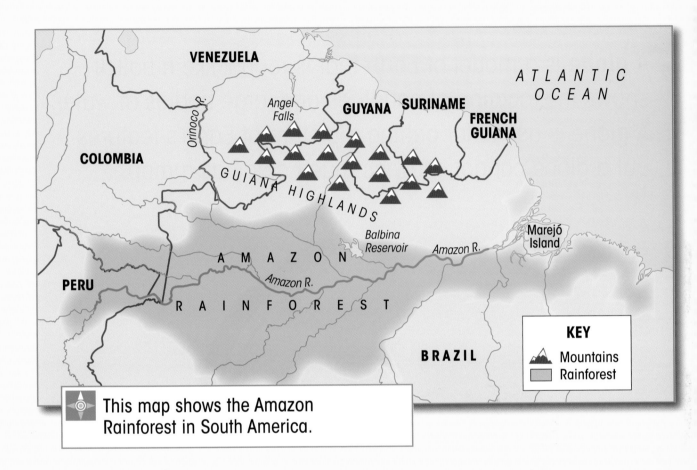

This map shows the Amazon
Rainforest in South America.

Maps teach us about the world. We can use them to find
the location of places. We can use them to study physical
features such as mountains or lakes. We can also use
maps to learn about people who live in different places
around the world.

Globes and Maps

A **globe** is a model of Earth that is round, like a ball. It shows the location of countries and large bodies of water. A globe is useful for getting a picture of Earth's features. But a globe cannot show as much detail as a map.

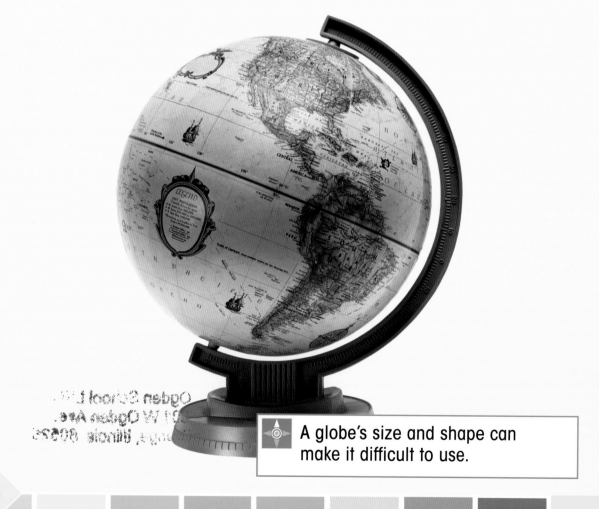

A globe's size and shape can make it difficult to use.

A map shows Earth's features on a flat surface. **Cartographers** change the shape and size of things on Earth. They do this do to fit the round Earth onto a flat map.

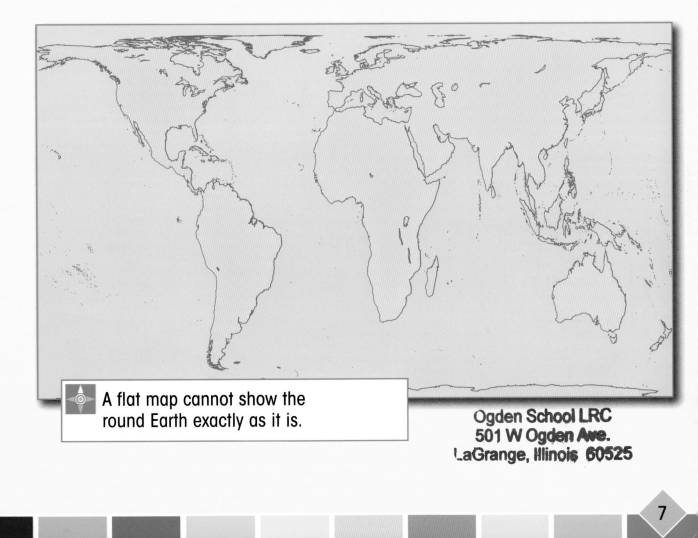

A flat map cannot show the round Earth exactly as it is.

Reading Maps

Maps have many features that help you read them. Most maps have a title that tells what the map is about. Maps also have a **key**. The key tells what the **symbols** on the map mean. Symbols are small pictures or shapes that stand for things in real life.

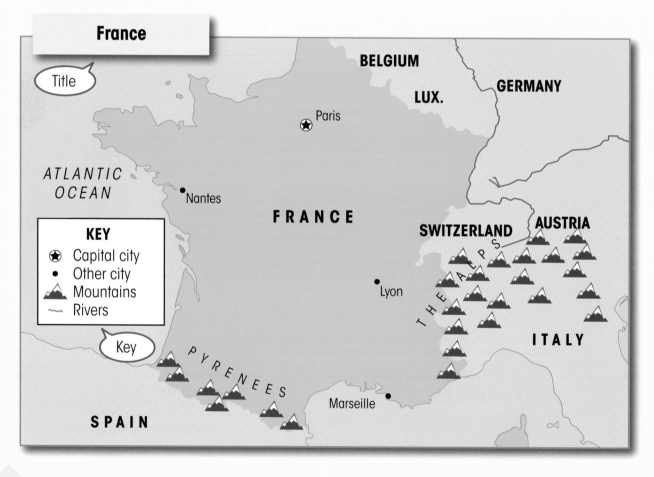

France

Title

BELGIUM

LUX.

GERMANY

Paris

ATLANTIC OCEAN

Nantes

FRANCE

SWITZERLAND

AUSTRIA

KEY
- ★ Capital city
- • Other city
- ⛰ Mountains
- ~ Rivers

Key

Lyon

THE ALPS

ITALY

PYRENEES

Marseille

SPAIN

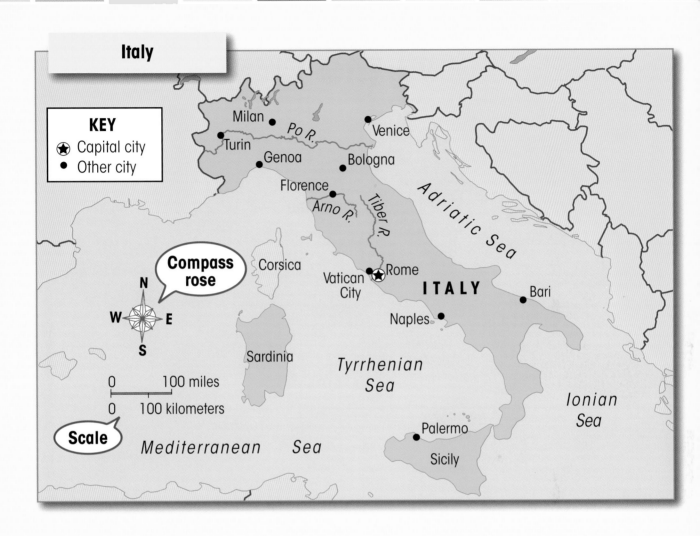

Italy

KEY
⭐ Capital city
● Other city

Milan
Po R.
Venice
Turin
Genoa
Bologna
Florence
Arno R.
Tiber R.
Adriatic Sea
Corsica
Compass rose
N
W E
S
Vatican City
Rome
ITALY
Bari
Naples
Sardinia
Tyrrhenian Sea
Ionian Sea
0   100 miles
0   100 kilometers
Scale
Palermo
Sicily
Mediterranean   Sea

The **compass rose** is a feature that shows direction. The four main directions are north, south, east, and west.

The **scale** is a feature that tells how far apart things are in real life. It shows how many miles or kilometers equal every inch or centimeter.

Lines around the World

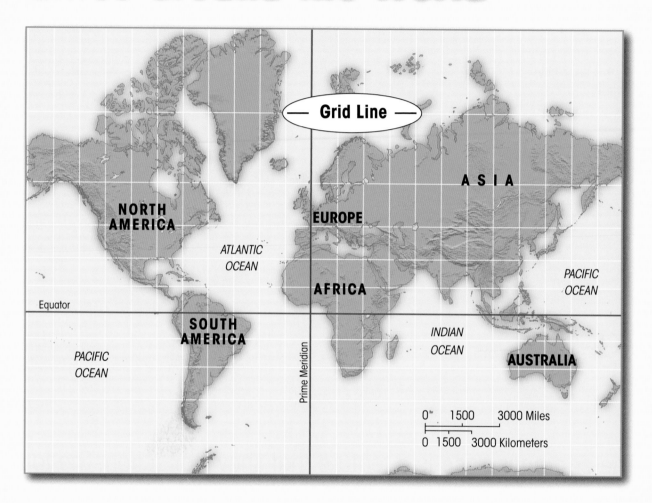

- Grid Line -

ASIA

NORTH
AMERICA

EUROPE

ATLANTIC
OCEAN

PACIFIC
OCEAN

AFRICA

Equator

SOUTH
AMERICA

INDIAN
OCEAN

PACIFIC
OCEAN

Prime Meridian

AUSTRALIA

0   1500   3000 Miles

0   1500   3000 Kilometers

Many maps have thin lines that look like a net thrown over the map. These are called **grid** lines. They can be used to find the location of places.

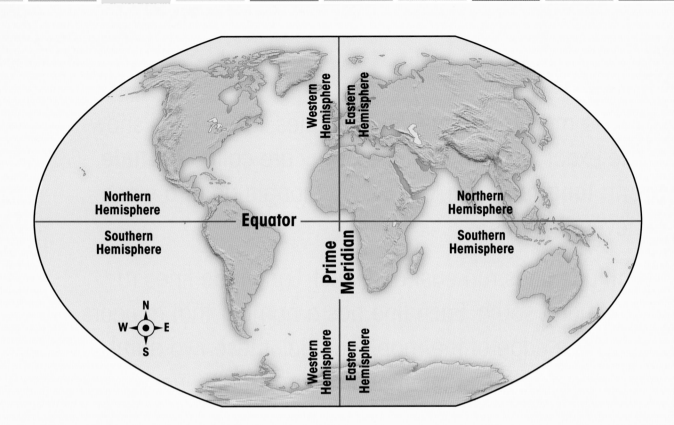

The **Equator** and the **Prime Meridian** are special grid lines. The Equator is halfway between the North Pole and South Pole. It divides the world into two halves, or **hemispheres**. These are the Northern Hemisphere and Southern Hemisphere.

The Prime Meridian goes from the North Pole to the South Pole. The Prime Meridian also divides the world into the Eastern Hemisphere and Western Hemisphere.

Latitude and Longitude

Some maps have special **grid** lines. These lines show the exact location of places. They are called **latitude** and **longitude**. The latitude and longitude of a place never changes.

Latitude lines run east and west. Longitude lines run north and south. Each line has a number that appears near the edge of the map. Together, these two numbers show the exact location of any place in the world.

Look at the map on page 13. Can you use the lines to find the latitude and longitude of New York City?

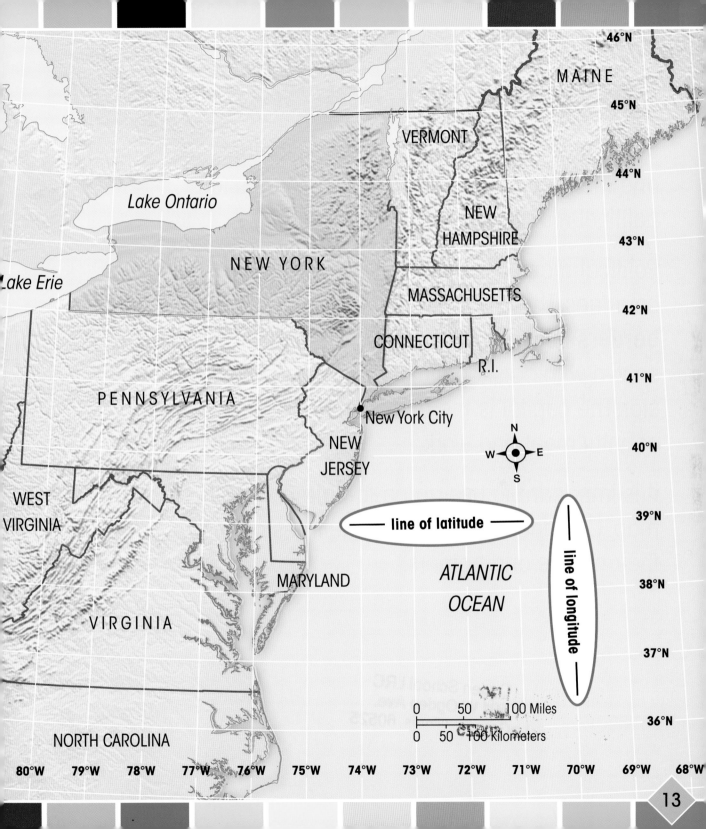

MAINE

46°N

45°N

VERMONT

44°N

NEW
HAMPSHIRE

43°N

Lake Ontario

NEW YORK

MASSACHUSETTS

42°N

Lake Erie

CONNECTICUT

41°N

R.I.

New York City

40°N

PENNSYLVANIA

NEW
JERSEY

N

W ● E

S

line of latitude

39°N

WEST
VIRGINIA

ATLANTIC
OCEAN

38°N

line of longitude

MARYLAND

37°N

VIRGINIA

0   50   100 Miles

36°N

0   50   100 Kilometers

NORTH CAROLINA

80°W   79°W   78°W   77°W   76°W   75°W   74°W   73°W   72°W   71°W   70°W   69°W   68°W

Maps about Countries

Some maps show the location of countries and their major cities. These maps are called political maps.

Political maps use color to show different countries. They use dark lines to show the **borders** between them. Cities are usually shown with dots. Capitals may be shown with a star. The capital is the place where leaders of a country meet and work.

It is important to use an up-to-date political map. Countries and states sometimes change their names and borders.

North America

Caribbean Sea

Caracas

VENEZUELA

—Orinoco River

Georgetown

Paramaribo

GUYANA

SURINAME

FRENCH GUIANA (FRANCE)

COLOMBIA

Bogotá

Quito

ECUADOR

Equator

Amazon River

Galápagos Islands (ECUADOR)

ANDES MOUNTAINS

Country border lines

BRAZIL

PERU

Lima

PACIFIC OCEAN

La Paz

BOLIVIA

Sucre

Brasília

Paraná River

Lake Titicaca

Rio de Janeiro

PARAGUAY

Asunción

São Paulo

Atacama Desert

0   400   800 Miles

0   400   800 Kilometers

ANDES MOUNTAINS

CHILE

Santiago

URUGUAY

Montevideo

Buenos Aires

ATLANTIC OCEAN

ARGENTINA

KEY

✪ Capital City

● Major City

Falkland Islands (UNITED KINGDOM)

15

Maps about Land

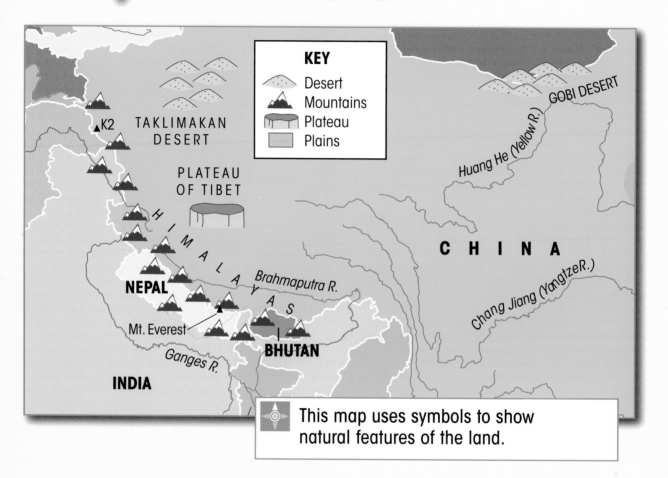

KEY
- Desert
- Mountains
- Plateau
- Plains

K2
TAKLIMAKAN DESERT
PLATEAU OF TIBET
HIMALAYAS
NEPAL
Mt. Everest
Ganges R.
INDIA
BHUTAN
Brahmaputra R.
CHINA
Huang He (Yellow R.)
GOBI DESERT
Chang Jiang (Yangtze R.)

This map uses symbols to show natural features of the land.

Physical maps show the natural features of a place. They can show mountains, deserts, and plains. Some physical maps use **symbols** to show these features.

Some physical maps use different colors to show high and low places. On the map below, brown shows areas where the land is high, such as mountain ranges. Light green shows areas where the land is low.

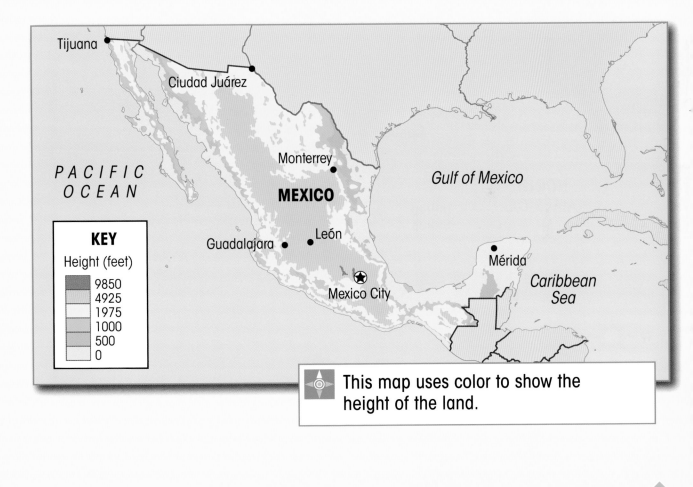

Tijuana

Ciudad Juárez

PACIFIC
OCEAN

Monterrey

Gulf of Mexico

MEXICO

KEY

Height (feet)

	9850
	4925
	1975
	1000
	500
	0

Guadalajara

León

Mérida

Caribbean
Sea

Mexico City

This map uses color to show the height of the land.

Maps about Water

Many physical maps show Earth's bodies of water. You can use them to locate oceans, lakes, and rivers. Water is almost always shown with the color blue.

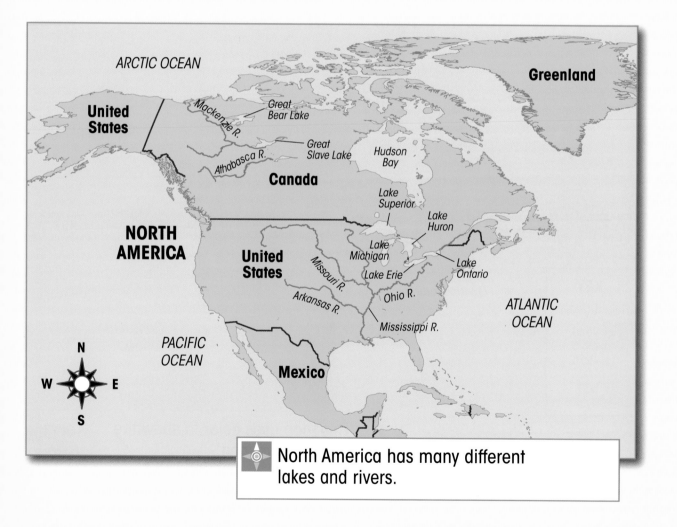

North America has many different lakes and rivers.

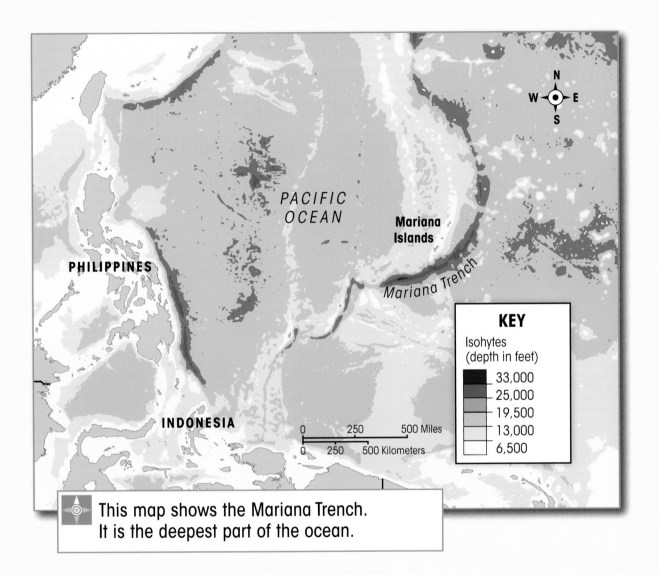

PACIFIC OCEAN

Mariana Islands

Mariana Trench

PHILIPPINES

INDONESIA

| 0 | 250 | 500 Miles |
| 0 | 250 | 500 Kilometers |

KEY

Isohytes
(depth in feet)

33,000
25,000
19,500
13,000
6,500

This map shows the Mariana Trench.
It is the deepest part of the ocean.

Some physical maps show what lies underneath the water.
Some parts of the ocean have mountains and valleys, just
as on land. Maps can also show how deep the water is.

Maps about Climate

Climate is the usual weather a place gets over a long period of time. Places in the world have different climates. Some places are hot and dry most of the year. Some places are cold, and some places are wet.

Can you find these climates on the map on the next page?

Many climate maps use color to show different climates. It is important to look at the **key** to see what the colors stand for.

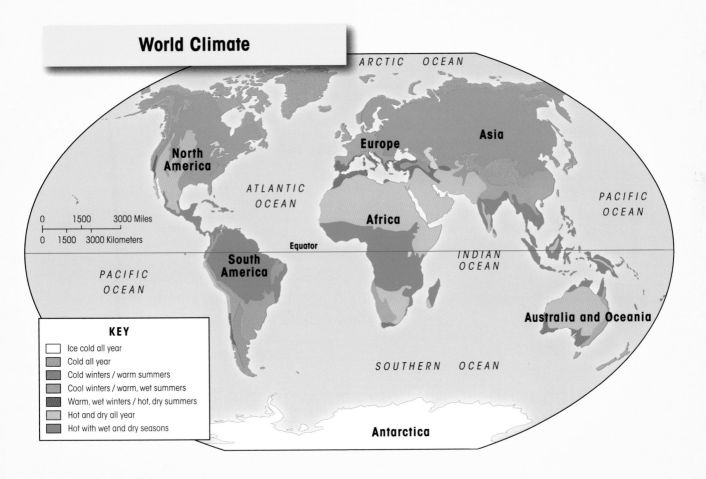

World Climate

ARCTIC OCEAN

Asia

Europe

North America

ATLANTIC OCEAN

PACIFIC OCEAN

Africa

0   1500   3000 Miles
0   1500   3000 Kilometers

Equator

INDIAN OCEAN

South America

PACIFIC OCEAN

Australia and Oceania

SOUTHERN OCEAN

KEY
- Ice cold all year
- Cold all year
- Cold winters / warm summers
- Cool winters / warm, wet summers
- Warm, wet winters / hot, dry summers
- Hot and dry all year
- Hot with wet and dry seasons

Antarctica

Maps about People

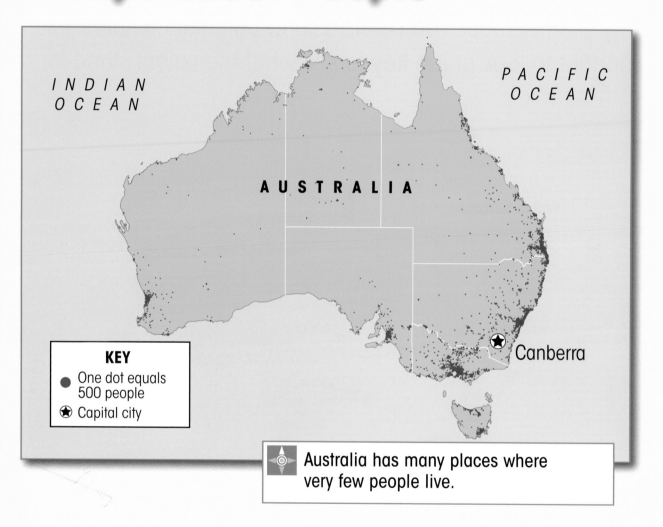

INDIAN
OCEAN

PACIFIC
OCEAN

AUSTRALIA

KEY
- One dot equals 500 people
- ⭐ Capital city

⭐ Canberra

Australia has many places where very few people live.

Population maps show how many people live in an area. The population map above uses dots to show population.

Some population maps use color to show how many people live in an area. The map **key** tells how many people are shown by each color.

Population of the United Kingdom

KEY
People per sq. mile

- 0–2.5
- 2.5–12.5
- 12.5–62.5
- 62.5–250
- 250–1,250
- 1,250–2,500
- Over 2,500

ATLANTIC OCEAN

SCOTLAND

Glasgow
Edinburgh

NORTHERN IRELAND

Belfast

UNITED KINGDOM

North Sea

Dublin

Irish Sea

IRELAND

Liverpool
Manchester

WALES

Birmingham

ENGLAND

Celtic Sea

Cardiff

London

Maps about the Economy

A country's **economy** is all the things it makes, sells, and buys. Economic maps can show what types of jobs people have. They also show what foods they grow and what things they make and sell.

Land Use in Brazil

VENEZUELA
GUYANA
SURINAME
FRENCH GUIANA
COLOMBIA
ECUADOR
ATLANTIC OCEAN
• Belém
PERU
BRAZIL
PACIFIC OCEAN
BOLIVIA
⭐ Brasilia
PARAGUAY
• Rio de Janiero
ARGENTINA

KEY
Farming
Livestock raising
Forestry
Trade and manufacturing
⭐ Capital city
• Other cities

This map uses color to show ways people use the land in the country Brazil.

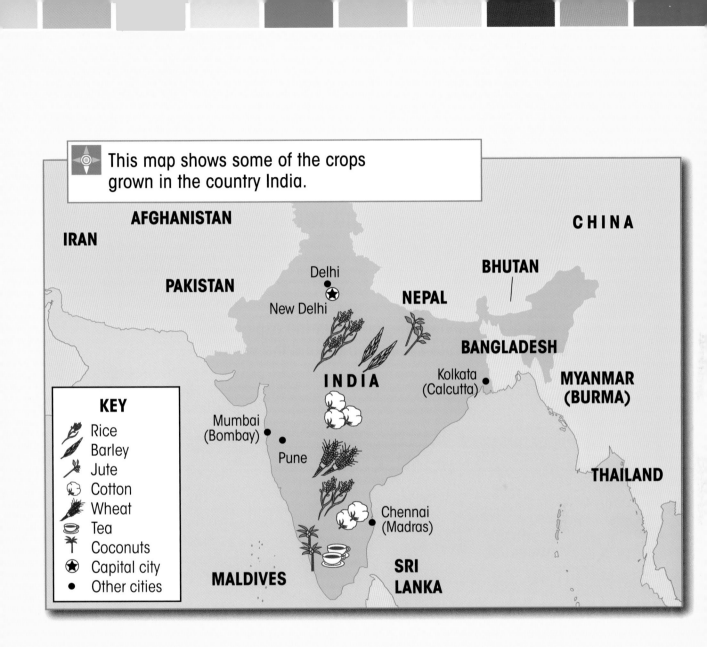

This map shows some of the crops grown in the country India.

AFGHANISTAN

IRAN

CHINA

PAKISTAN

Delhi

New Delhi

NEPAL

BHUTAN

BANGLADESH

INDIA

Kolkata
(Calcutta)

MYANMAR
(BURMA)

Mumbai
(Bombay)

Pune

THAILAND

Chennai
(Madras)

MALDIVES

SRI
LANKA

KEY

Rice
Barley
Jute
Cotton
Wheat
Tea
Coconuts
Capital city
Other cities

Some maps show what types of **crops** are grown in an area. These maps often use **symbols** instead of colors.

Maps about History

Historical maps tell us what the world used to be like. They also show what people knew about the world. Some historical maps show the **route** that people took to reach new places.

This historical map shows the route that the explorer Ferdinand Magellan took on his trip around the world.

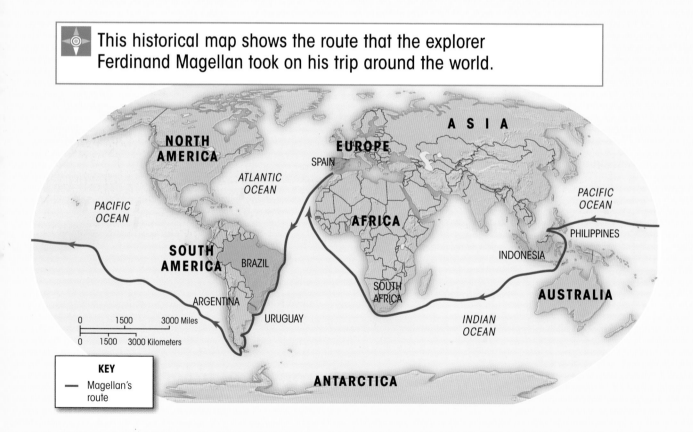

NORTH AMERICA

ATLANTIC OCEAN

PACIFIC OCEAN

SOUTH AMERICA

BRAZIL

ARGENTINA

URUGUAY

0   1500   3000 Miles
0   1500   3000 Kilometers

EUROPE

SPAIN

ASIA

AFRICA

SOUTH AFRICA

INDIAN OCEAN

PACIFIC OCEAN

PHILIPPINES

INDONESIA

AUSTRALIA

ANTARCTICA

KEY
— Magellan's route

With maps, we can learn all kinds of things about the world. The world continues to change, and maps help us keep up with these changes.

Map Activities

The Great Circle Route

For this activity you will need:

- a large world map
- a **globe**
- small pieces of tape
- one or two long pieces of string

1. On a world map, find the United States. Now find the state of Illinois. Then find the city of Chicago.

2. Now find Europe on the map. Find the country of Italy. Now find the city of Rome.

3. Tape one end of the string onto Chicago and the other end of the string on Rome. Write down the names of all the cities that your string passes through.

4. Next, do the same thing on a globe. Tape one end of the string to Rome, and one to Chicago. Follow the same path you did on the map along the same line of **latitude**. Make sure you go through the same cities on the globe that you did on the map.

Is this the shortest route between the two cities? Using the globe, find the shortest route. Which route passes the nearest to the North Pole and South Pole?

See if you can find two other cities that are directly east and west of each other and repeat the activity.

Comparing Maps

1. Find a **population** map and a physical map of the same country. Check the **scale** to make sure the maps show the same size area.

2. Find the area with the most people. What are the natural features there?

3. Find the area with the fewest people. What are the natural features there? You will probably see that most people live close to rivers, and very few people live in deserts or very cold areas.

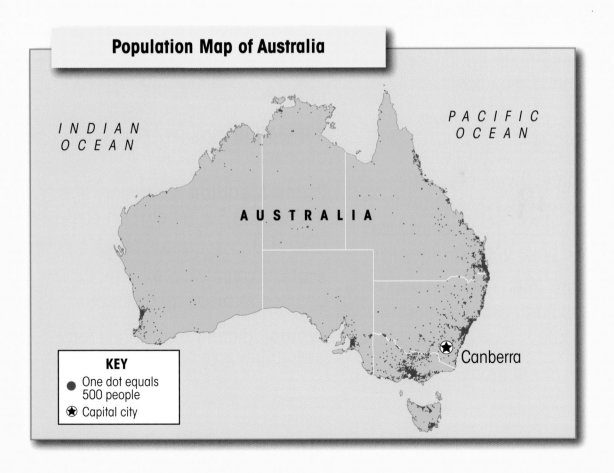

Population Map of Australia

INDIAN
OCEAN

PACIFIC
OCEAN

AUSTRALIA

Canberra

KEY
- One dot equals 500 people
- ⊛ Capital city

Glossary

border imaginary line that divides two places

cartographer person who makes maps

climate usual weather in an area. The weather changes from day to day, but the climate stays the same.

compass rose symbol on a map that shows direction

crop plant that is grown by farmers

economy things a country grows, makes, buys, and sells. It also includes the kinds of jobs people have and how they live.

Equator imaginary line that divides Earth between north and south

globe round model of Earth

grid group of lines that are the same distance apart

hemisphere one half of Earth

key table that shows what the symbols on the map mean

latitude lines on a map or globe that run from east to west

longitude lines on a map or globe that run from north to south

population group or number of people

Prime Meridian imaginary line that divides Earth between east and west

scale feature on a map that can be used to measure distance

symbol picture that stands for something else

Find Out More

Organizations and Websites

The Websites below may have some advertisements on them. Make sure to ask a trusted adult to look at them with you. You should never give out personal information, including your name and address, without talking to a trusted adult.

National Geographic
National Geographic provides free maps and photos of Earth.
Visit **www.nationalgeographic.com**.

Yahoo Maps
Visit Yahoo maps (**www.maps.yahoo.com**) to find directions from your house to places nearby and far away. Try putting in your address and the address of your school. Do the directions given match your route?

Books to Read

Deboo, Ana. *Mapping the World*. Chicago: Heinemann Library, 2006.

Junior Classroom Atlas. Chicago: Rand McNally, 2001.

Mahaney, Ian F. *Political Maps*. New York: Rosen, 2007.

McKay, Sindy. *About the Seasons*. San Anselmo, CA: Treasure Bay, 2000.

Index